Are You *Still* Pregnant?
The dos and don'ts of pregnancy
for everyone involved

by
Mike Wellins and Gem Noland

No part of this publication may be reproduced in whole or in part, or stored in a retrieval system and transmitted in any form or by any means, electronic, mechanical, photocopying, recording or otherwise, without written permission by the publisher. For information regarding permission,
email Mike@freakybuttrue.com.

ISBN 978-1468103168

Text copyright © 1999 Mike Wellins
Illustrations and graphics
copyright © 1999 Mike Wellins

All rights reserved. Published by
Freakybuttrue
Portland, Oregon.

Printed in the USA

www.freakybuttrue.com

First things first

Calm down. Let's take a deep breath, and just relax. Isn't that better? Everything is going to be just fine. Now, if you're reading this book, then you, or some woman you know, close or not too close, is going to have a baby. In simple terms, pregnant, with child or expecting. Well rest assured, this lttle book is here to help. Pregnancy is a long and complicated process, with the full range of feelings and emotions. Birth is a great big deal and inarguably a major player in our civilization and life as we know it.

Life is being born a billion times a day on every level, from microbes to yuppies. Be that as it may, if you have never been pregnant, or you are close to the woman with "the bun in the oven"* then you are in for an unforgettable experience.

Legal Jargon:

This book is for entertainment and humor relief only. No medical diagnosis or medical treatment should be inferred. None of the jokes or gags here are to be taken more seriously than reading humor. At most, this book is a strong suggestion for pregnant women, their partners and families to do loads of thorough research into the whole birth process, including consulting with doctors and other qualified medical professionals.

* Generally, pregnant women don't care for the term, "Bun in the Oven".

Either way, this doesn't mean that you can't have a little fun with it. So sit back, relax, remember to breathe, and consult this manual regularly. This book may (or may not) help ease the bumps, no matter which side of the big belly you may be on.

And don't feel too bad; elephants are pregnant for 22 months.

Soon there will be a whole new person; the baby, another runner in the race of civilization with all the ramifications therein. But this isn't about the shiny new citizen on the way, there will be plenty of time for oogling over babies. This book is about the shockwaves that emit from the pre-baby epicenter that affects all that get in range, including mom herself, friends, family, pets, plants, dwellings and structures.

This book is for immediate use in moderate doses. Before using any drugs, therapy, friendly advice, pamphlet, videocasette, books on tape, or mantra, consult your physician, oracle, tarot, psychic or shaman.

Don't even go there

During pregnancy, every part of a woman's body can be a potential emotional hot spot. Using this diagram, try to avoid these and similar questions and phrases.

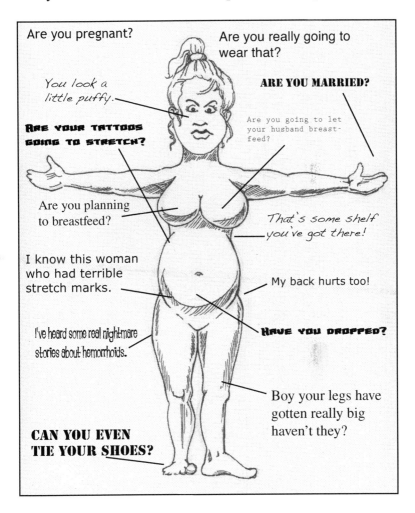

With pregnancy comes some inevitable changes in a woman's physiology and many of them aren't that comfortable. Early on, and also considered to be one of the first real benchmarks of pregnancy is the often noted getting sick, barfing, hurling, puking, or vomiting. Almost unavoidable, there are few considerations that can make barfing less of a drag. The best you can try for is a sense of timing. If you find yourself in the barfing phase, try to plan your day accordingly, and remember these two crucial words: **barf bag**.

Simple, yet effective. Get a few.

The worst places to barf

The bath

A train or car

A roadside gas station sink

The movies, a funeral or other social function.

Great places to barf

Off a building

Cozy at home, in a clean bathroom with candles.

Off a pier or dock

Don't get cocky either; it's never ok to use barfing as a weapon, unless it's in self-defense.

With all these random variables, it is certain that tempers will flare and mistakes will be made. Either precautionary or retroactively, nothing works better to grease the wheels of biology than a little gift-giving. A gift is an age-old symbol of feelings and often in this situation, sympathy. Still, like everything else in this unpredictable time, use caution and common sense.

Good gifts for a pregnant woman

- Magic Powers
- Comfortable Shoes
- Tissue
- Video Coupons
- Massage Gift Certificates

Bad gifts for a pregnant woman

- Lingerie
- Roller blades
- Free passes to **Metallica**
- Scarves
- A T-shirt that reads: "Big is beautiful"
- Balloon gags

Listen up and/or shut up

Fluctuations in hormones seem to have an amplifying effect on the woman's ear, but more particularly the impact of the statement. The following statements have been tested for years and are surefire hits when it comes to really pissing off a pregnant woman. This book recommends eliminating them from your vocabulary.

👎 "How much do you weigh now?"

👎 "Was it planned?"

👎 "I hear that birth is the most painful experience a woman can have."

👎 "Are you getting cravings for pickles and ice cream?"

"Are you <u>still</u> pregnant?"

👎 "Did you have your baby yet?"

👎 "I've been really tired lately, too."

👎 "Are you really going to wear that?"

👎 "Can I touch your belly?"

Hey there little lady! Gettin' pretty big there."

Things not to say to a pregnant woman

👎 "Who's the father?"
👎 "Are you married?"
👎 "I'll bet your husband is excited!"

"Maybe it will be twins!?"

👎 "Did you know that college will cost a thousand dollars a second in 18 years?"
👎 "You must be _____ months."
👎 "You are so small for _____ months."
👎 "Oh, you are really big for _____ months."
👎 "Don't go into labor now!"

"Whoa, is that a kid in there or what?"

👎"I thought that you were going to wait..?.."
👎"Hey! Looks like you've been busy."
👎"Thar she blows!"
Avoid all whale or elephant comparisons.

Not since Melville have whale metaphors been met with such intensity. By and large, animal comparisons of any nature are ill-advised.*

*Except when using one to punctuate that very topic with an inocuous cartoon...whew...that was close.

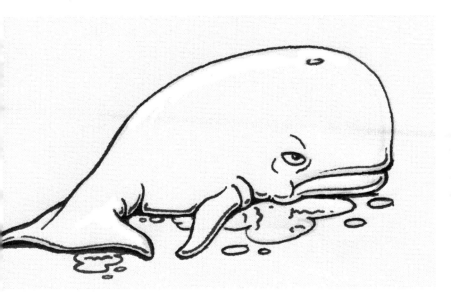

Just trying to help

Depending on the precise moment, there are things you can say that will be greeted with delight when presented to a pregnant woman.

Possible good things to say to a pregnant woman:

- 👍 I'll be back in a while.
- 👍 Let's order some pizza!
- 👍 More pizza coming!
- 👍 You look fantastic!
- 👍 Do you want me to rub your back?
- 👍 Lookie! Ice cream and a video!
- 👍 Lets go for a walk.
- 👍 Let's sit down.
- 👍 I'll put on some music.
- 👍 I'll drive your parents to the airport.

Trying too hard

Conversely, variables may fluctuate and phrases that were so helpful and friendly not seconds ago, now land on the pregnant woman's ears like an aircraft carrier on a chalk board.

Possible bad things to say to a pregnant woman:

- 👎 Good morning.
- 👎 How are you doing?
- 👎 Let's stay in.
- 👎 Let's go out.
- 👎 Do you want me to rub your back?
- 👎 You look hot!
- 👎 You don't look so hot.
- 👎 Let's sit down.
- 👎 Can I get you anything?
- 👎 Your folks are here.

Remarkably the process of birth triggers reactions in the woman, what is known as <u>Every Woman for Herself Procedure</u> or **EWFHP**.

I'm due in two weeks!

So strong is this reaction that a woman in the throes of a full pregnancy can turn on any other woman who is going or has gone through the same process.

Advice

Normally an individual might appreciate the advice of a peer or an elder who has undergone s strenuous event. Often, advice from previous mothers to the new mother are the key to smoothly traversing the pregnancy landscape. Other times, the same advice comes at a high cost. Here are some advice samples that any person close to the pregnant woman might consider rephrasing or avoiding:

"I was only in labor for 5 minutes!"

"Don't worry, it's worth it!"

"I WAS SICK THE WHOLE TIME."

"It's really going to change your life."

You will feel better after the third month.

"I only gained fifteen pounds."

"Are you sure you want to eat that?"

"What kind of birth are you having?"

"You really have that glow."

A few words about mom's mom

The world and the universe are governed by physics. Everything must conform to the rules, and the sensitive mother and pregnant daughter relationship is no exception. Similar to charged atoms, this relationship can operate in a wildly erratic manner known as the reversible dynamic principle (RDP).

At times the mom and the new mom are positively charged and form a strong bond. Instantly, however, situations can arise: helping too much, not helping enough, not offering enough suggestions, offering too many sugestions, hinting, nodding, pointing and a million other variables can cause one of the mom's polarity to change. Although not fully explained, the moms begin to repel each other in a drastic way. Try and pay close attention to the charge and avoid serious shock.

When I was carryin' your daddy, I was in hard labor for the better part of three weeks, course I was still working seven jobs. And when my water finally did break I thought I'd given birth to Flipper!

Similarly, stature and range can also have little to no effect. Advice once considered wise and invaluable now sounds like a series of insults strung together.

The family

Inarguably, without pregnancy there is no family. We all came from families of one sort or another and in certain instances the family can be a pillar of support and comfort.

Still, in this choppy sea of emotions, that same family can unintentionally become a source of great stress, anger and volatility by the simple act of showing up.

One of the major ideas here is to alleviate stress and make the whole pregnancy as easy as possible. It is important that the family and the mother gauge the relationship on a moment-to-moment basis, and in worst case scenarios, put distance between the two potentially hostile parties.

It's not all bad
Still in all, this age-old process does have some benefits to help level the field. Positive and fun perks can and should be exploited to their limit.

Good things about being pregnant
Pregnancy is the greatest, iron-clad excuse to avoid social stuff and cancel plans on a dime.

Call it what you will: Major boobs, mounds of plenty, hooterville's population explosion, here comes the dairy, or just big jugs.

Regardless of the name, it all comes back to fabulous cleavage! (results may vary.)

Good things about being pregnant

A silky, shiny coat

(hair growth and silkiness may vary.)

Good things about being pregnant

For a brief, short, shining moment, a woman's weight goes out the window.

Sure it's corny, but here comes Super Horny!

Things you'll never find so stop looking

A comfortable chair

Maternity swim-suit.

Underwear that doesn't look like gramma's

𝒜 non-nauseating 𝒯hai or 𝒞hinese restaurant.

Short enough movies.

Things that usually suck

CIGARETTES.

COLOGNE

Incense

SOAP STORES

A distant due date

BRATTY KIDS

Burp smell

LEFTOVERS

Miscellaneous things to watch out for

Gas pains that feel like birth.

For Christmas: baby stuff and baby stuff only.

The world's supply of movie theater popcorn

Inescapable basket chairs.

Spiral staircases.

A word about hot flashes:
There are no preparateions required; they will come, they will be numerous.

A word about thighs

A lot will be said about a pregnant woman's legs, thighs and butt and that is precisely the problem. Nothing should be said on that subject. The general woman's diagram earlier in the book discusses thighs briefly as an area non grata, but its level of importance is such that it requires a full page. Never mention a pregnant woman's leg growth. Never use words like: ballooning, stuffed or swollen in any paragraph that has anything to do with her legs, rear or thighs.

Even if asked, remember that honesty is good, but the truth hurts, and in this case, the truth can break teeth and ribs. If a pregnant woman were to ask about her thighs, legs, or butt, it is acceptable to:

❏ Change the subject.

❏ Hide.

❏ Feign a phone call or page.

❏ Suddenly leave the room because you realize that the car's emergency brake might not be set.

Take it easy

As you and your baby grow, you will become more adept at getting around. That's good. Getting over-confident is bad. Because while while you're getting acclimated, you're still getting bigger. Always allow plenty of room in clothes, cars, and doorways. Get plenty of doctor approved exercise but don't overdo it. All the extra weight can also make your back much more easily strained, so try to remember you're a wide load for a while.

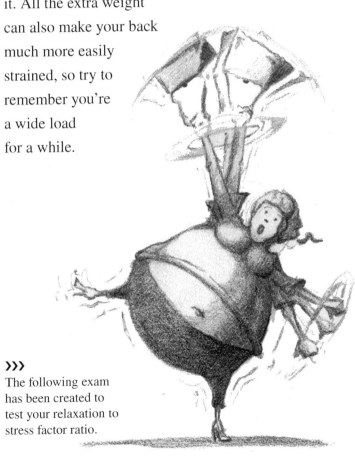

>>>
The following exam has been created to test your relaxation to stress factor ratio.

26354/65.224 rev. 42

EWPTDA

SHORT FORM A

Early Warning Pregnancy Test and Diagnostic Analysis
This test is designed to test individuals and pregnant mothers with a battery of questions that if answered wrong could bring to light certain weaknesses in the testee's pregnancy knowledge.

Stop!

Wait!.... Not yet. Answer the questions as honestly as possible. Before starting, pick up <u>only</u> a No. 2 pencil and sharpen it. No cheating or looking up the answers. You have 34 mintues. When you've finished, raise your hand, close your test and put your head down on your desk. Ok, not yet.... wait for it.....

Get ready...

Begin.

1. Smoking while pregnant has proven to be:
- A. Fun and fancy!
- B. Disasterous to the infant's health and birth weight.
- C. No longer hip.
- D. Idiotic
- E. B, C and D

GO ON TO THE NEXT PAGE, IF YOU WANT.

2. A pregnant woman is riding on a train from Des Moines, Iowa at 60 miles per hour. A pregnant woman is riding a train from Winnamucca, Nevada at 73 miles per hour. Simultaneously, the two women see two different poignant billboards about rug cleaning and start sobbing. They did this because:

A. They're just like that.
B. They're faking.
C. They've gone a little fingaling pingy.
D. Chemical changes can cause drastic emotional fluctuations.
E. Not A but D

3. When attending a baby shower _____.

A. Wear a slicker as to not get wet in the shower
B. Don't expect male strippers.
C. Point a lot at the mother-to-be and say, "Whoa, Fuji blimp, where's the football game tonight?"
D. Be supportive and have a nice time.
E. Don't discuss movies like *Rosemary's Baby* and *It's Alive*.

DO NOT WRITE BELOW THIS LINE

Ok, if you really have to write here, and can't find anyplace else, go ahead. Then go on to the next page...if you want.

4. If a pregnant woman is angry and asks you to go away, what should you do?

- [ ] A. Stay around, and try to discuss which faults of yours are so annoying.
- [ ] B. Suggest a board game.
- [ ] C. Argue and go off on petty tangents.
- [ ] D. Go away, but then come right back in an try to discuss "issues".
- [ ] E. Go away.

5. Pregnant women should chop wood or build a deck:

- [ ] A. All of the time
- [ ] B. Some of the time
- [ ] C. Occasionally
- [ ] D. Rarely
- [ ] E. Never

6. Three pregnant women are standing side by side outside a seafood restaurant. The first woman barfs 3 feet, the next woman barfs 5 feet and the third barfs 2 feet. Which woman had the salmon mousse?

- [ ] A. Woman One
- [ ] B. Woman Two
- [ ] C. Woman Three
- [ ] D. B
- [ ] E. D

Enjoy the cartoon. When finished go on to the next page...if you want.

7. Humoring an extra cranky pregnant woman is a good idea:

- A. All of the time.
- B. All of the time.
- C. All of the time.
- D. All of the time.
- E. All of the time.

8. It is an excellent idea to limit your _____ as much as possible.

- A. Nude bungee jumping
- B. Stress
- C. Car stunts
- D. A, B and C
- E. B

9. As we know from our reading, at the end of pregnancy, comes birth. Considering this major life changing event, it is important to:

- A. Set the VCR so as not to miss the good shows.
- B. Have important numbers of doctors, relatives, and friends on hand.
- C. Have a travel bag handy, a plan, and a working vehicle or viable transportation.
- D. Have a backup plan, backup transportation, and then back both of those up again.
- E. I'm sorry, what was the question?

**YOU'VE COMPLETED YOUR EXAM.
CHECK YOUR SCORE LATER IN THE BOOK.**

The clock is ticking

Your embryo is now making a trail through evolution; a single cell, a multicell, a zygote, a fish, a reptile, a mammal, a fetus, and finally a wet, new, pink, screaming, pooping baby. Early on, pregnant mothers will notice:

Tickling.

Tapping.

Poking.

KICKING.

Knocking.

Pounding.

Hammering.

Something that feels a lot like tunneling.

UNPROVOKED KICKS TO THE BLADDER

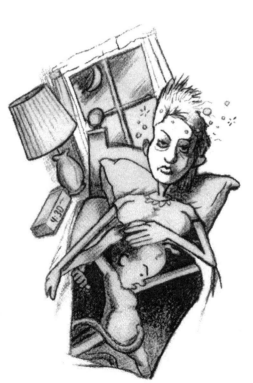

Coming into the home stretch

The bases are loaded and nobody knows this more than the pregnant mother. If she's wise, she will know that anything can happen and she'll be ready. Mom might be in a zone where she has grown fairly accustomed to her new way, and by the same token has had just about enough of it as well.

This isn't a contest

From the onset, a REASONABLE diet is found and stuck to. One of the most famous perks that goes with pregnancy is eating, and weight is not a major issue for a while, but again, consult a doctor about a healthy, proper diet. Serious weight gain can be serious.

Be prepared

The Boy Scouts have a great motto: Be prepared. Truly, a motto has never rung so true. Nature can be pushy, fickle and can also need help. When you go into labor this book officially ends, for you are no longer pregnant but are instead giving birth. Plan accordingly.

FUN FACT:
Winston Churchill was born in the bathroom at a dance.

Some studies suggest (you want the studies, you go find them) that the bonding of a child with Mommy are done very early in life; fetuses grow at an unbelievable speed, utilizing all the nutrients and chemicals that flow into them. Prolonged stress can cause chemical imbalances that could possibly influence lifelong traits.

It is then safe to say that any strong chemical, caffeine, cigarette smoke, alcohol, drugs and of course violence could and would have many bad consequences.

Also avoid any doses of industrial chemicals.

Remember that on the whole, relaxing is the key and relaxing is what mom and anyone else nearby can help out with. If someone or some situation is stressing out a pregnant woman, then that woman needs to distance herself from these stress points straight away, rude or not. Some stress is inevitable, but the more it can be minimized, the better. There will be plenty of time for stressing in the years to come: school, dating, college, to name a few. For nine months, mom-to-be is a stress free zone.

| Answers to the test questions: | **1.** B, C, D, E | **2.** D or E | **3.** B, D, E |
| **4.** E | **5.** E | **6.** C | **7.** A, B, C, D, E | **8.** D | **9.** B, C, D |

Warm baths, calmness, the ocean, swimming, resting, and even Mozart may be a factor in creating a cool kid. This book is about pregnancy so it is important to mention the heaps of recent research being done this very minute someplace. Right now, a bunch of serious guys with some great microscopes are learning more and more about early human development. These scientists have learned that developmentally, the earliest stages of life may be the most important, next to getting a driver's license.

Every new mother and family should make a serious commitment to learn what steps they can take to ensure proper fetus, baby, and finally child development.

Do not substitute this book for research: it is a very slim summary of the complex nature of pregnancy. Find books by reputable doctors and learn about what it takes to give your new child, a whole new person, the best possible chances to be an above-average individual. And as always, see a qualified medical doctor, and listen to what the doctor says, and if you are in doubt, get a second opinion.

Now what?

Pregnancy is to a woman what 45 London busses are to a motorcycle jumper. It's a big challenge, and it's not to be taken lightly. Once you start rolling, you've got one heck of a ride that will be exciting, but could also prove disasterous if not done right.

And when you've landed on the other side with your new baby, try to carry the determination of your birth through to a lifetime of child rearing and caring. And unlike the motorcycle jump, you can find plenty of qualified people to help you every step of the way and you probably won't break every bone in your body...

And if you feel more comfortable you can leave the helmet on.

*This book is
lovingly presented to:*

_____

on

_____

by

_____

Other Books by Mike Wellins:

What a World: The art of Colin Batty

Mountain of the Dead

Photographer Unknown

Serious Wackos

101 Things to do Besides Blowing Someone Away

Stella's Babysitting Service

Lightspeed Ahead

Chico Tubing Guide

www.freakybuttrue.com

Made in the USA
Middletown, DE
23 July 2022